Look and See 2

Susannah Reed

NATIONAL GEOGRAPHIC
LEARNING

Australia • Brazil • Mexico • Singapore • United Kingdom • United States

Scope and Sequence

How old are you? p. 4 — *Numbers 1–10; Aa, Ee, Ii, Oo, Uu*
How old are you? I'm four.

Unit		Words	Structure	Value	Letters and Sounds	Content Connections	Video	Project
1 At school p. 5		*blocks* *friend* *teacher* *felt tips* *glue* *paper* *scissors*	*Who's this?* *He's my grandpa.* *She's my friend.*	Be tidy in the classroom.	Bb /b/ Pp /p/	Engineering	Why do we play with building blocks?	A building block painting
2 Are you happy? p. 11		*happy* *angry* *excited* *hungry* *sad* *sleepy* *thirsty*	*Are you happy?* *Yes, I am.* *Are you sad?* *No, I'm not.*	Get a good night's sleep.	Dd /d/ Tt /t/	Music, Social Science	How does music make us feel?	A feelings mask
3 Animals p. 17		*owl* *bat* *bear* *duck* *fox* *rabbit* *snake*	*What is it?* *It's an owl.* *What are they?* *They're bears.*	Be curious about animals.	Ss /s/ Zz /z/	Science	What animals do we see at night and in the day?	A day and night scene
4 Get dressed p. 23		*scarf* *boots* *coat* *dress* *jumper* *skirt* *trousers*	*This is my jumper.* *These are my trousers.*	Dress for the weather.	Ll /l/ Rr /r/	Social Science	What clothes are made of cotton and silk?	A dressing-up doll
5 I can jump! p. 29		*jump* *crawl* *dance* *hop* *run* *turn around* *walk*	*I can hop.*	Play outside.	Mm /m/ Nn /n/	Physical Education	What can we do at a playground?	A playground

						Content Connections	
		Words	Structure	Value	Letters and Sounds	Video	Project
6 **Faces** p. 35		*face* *ears* *eyes* *hair* *mouth* *nose* *long* *short*	*He's got brown eyes.* *She's got long hair.*	Say nice things.	Gg /g/ Hh /h/	Science How do we use our senses?	A sensory box
7 **My things** p. 41		*dinosaur* *bike* *kite* *puzzle* *robot* *scooter* *tablet*	*Is this your kite?* *Yes, it is./* *No, it isn't.*	Take turns.	Cc /k/ Qq /kw/	History, Science What were dinosaurs like?	A fossil
8 **Babies** p. 47		*baby* *calf* *chick* *kitten* *lamb* *puppy* *big* *small*	*There's one cow.* *There are two calves.*	Be kind.	Kk /k/ Xx /ks/	Science What animals come from eggs?	An animal hatching picture
9 **What's for dinner?** p. 53		*dinner* *beans* *bread* *chicken* *fish* *noodles* *rice* *salad*	*What do you want?* *I want chicken, please.*	Help in the kitchen.	Jj /dʒ/ Yy /j/	Social Science How do we make noodle soup?	A noodle soup craft
10 **Insects** p. 59		*butterfly* *ant* *bee* *caterpillar* *ladybird* *snail* *spider*	*Where's the caterpillar?* *It's on an apple.*	Be kind to nature.	Ff /f/ Vv /v/ Ww /w/	Science What is the life cycle of a butterfly?	A butterfly life cycle diagram

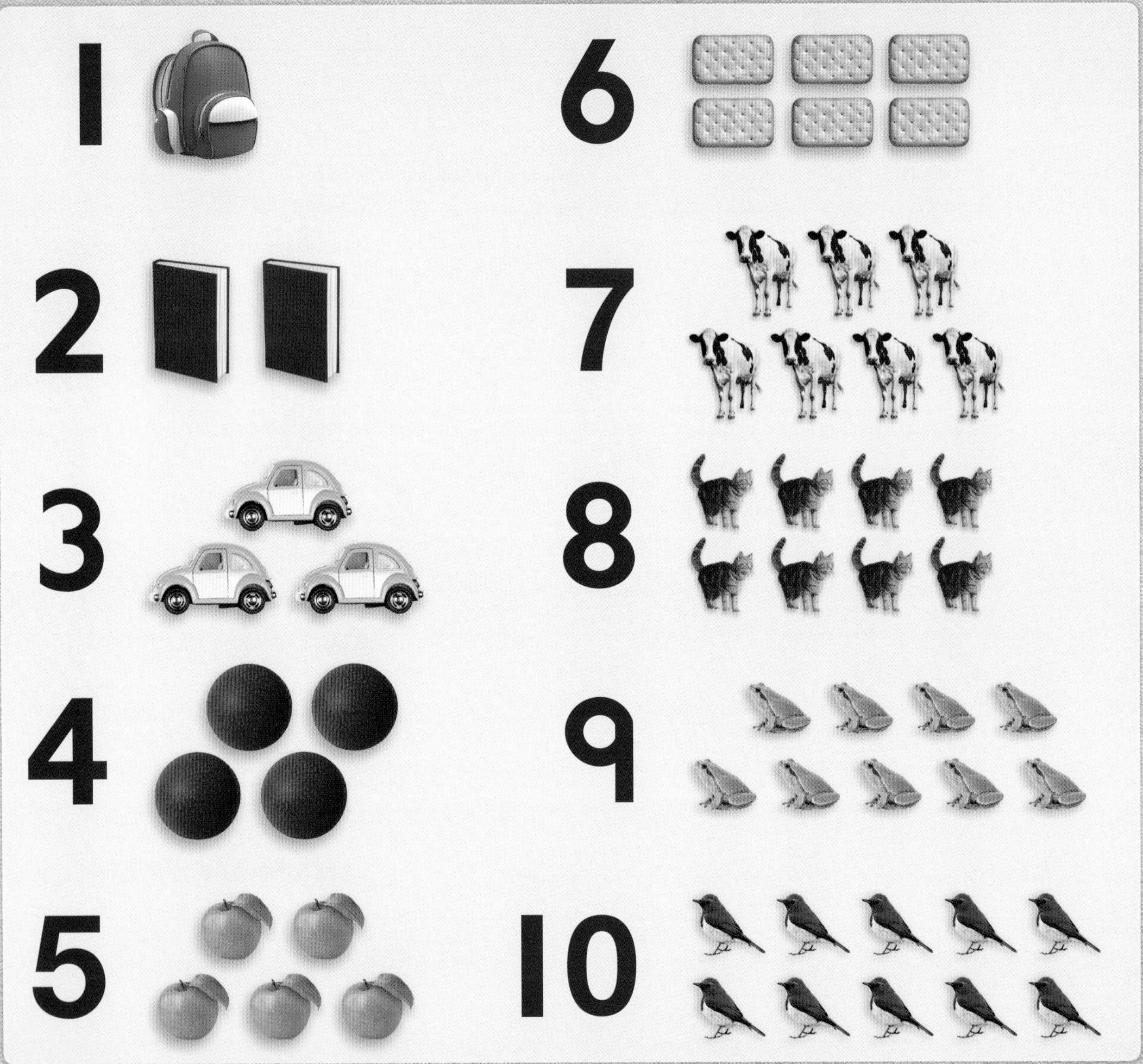

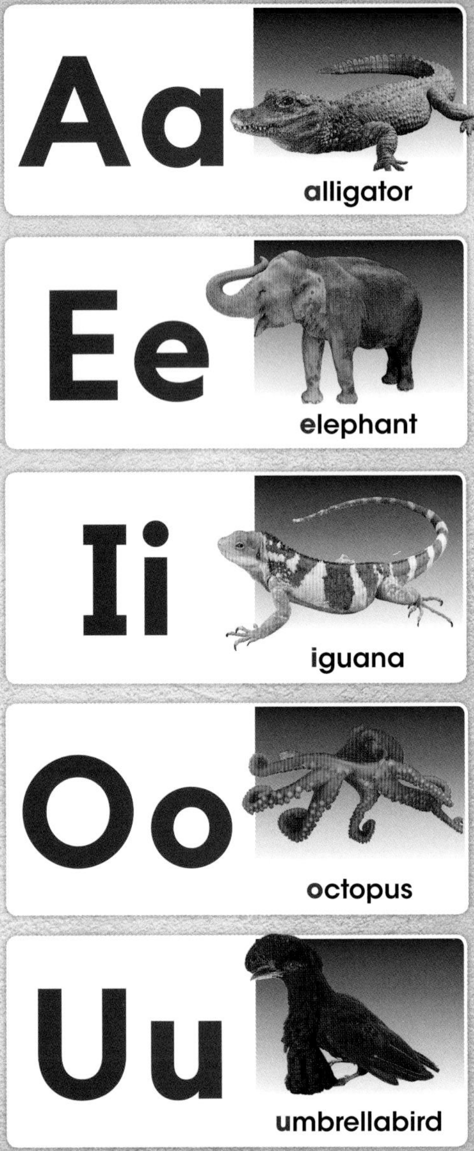

REVIEW: Numbers 1–10; Aa, Ee, Ii, Oo, Uu **STRUCTURE:** *How old are you? I'm four.*

1 TR: 0.1 Listen and chant. **2** TR: 0.2 Listen and say. **3** TR: 0.3 Listen, point and say.

Girls building with blocks, Egypt

LESSON 1

NEW WORD: *blocks*

1 Look and see. **2** SC: 1 Watch. **3** TR: 1.1 Listen and say. **4** TR: 1.2 Listen and do.

Children drawing at school, USA

LESSON 2

NEW WORDS: *friend, teacher; felt tips, glue, paper, scissors*

1 TR: 1.3 Listen and point. **2** TR: 1.4 Listen and say. **3** TR: 1.5 Listen and chant. **4** Find and say.

LESSON 3

STRUCTURE: *Who's this? He's my grandpa. She's my friend.*

1 TR: 1.6 Listen and follow. **2** TR: 1.7 Listen and say. **3** Play and say.

Girls at school, UAE

Think! Value

Be tidy in the classroom.

LESSON 4

SONG AND VALUE: *Be tidy in the classroom.*

1 TR: 1.8 Listen and point. **2** TR: 1.9 Listen and sing. **3** TR: 1.10 Sing and do. **4** Stick.

Bb

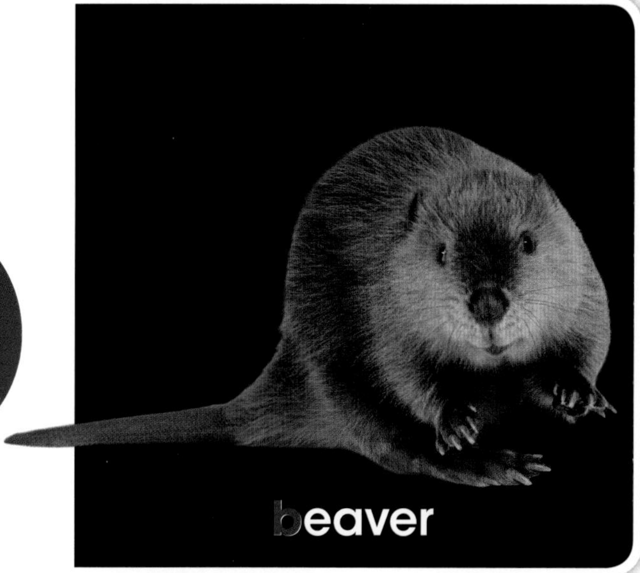

Pp

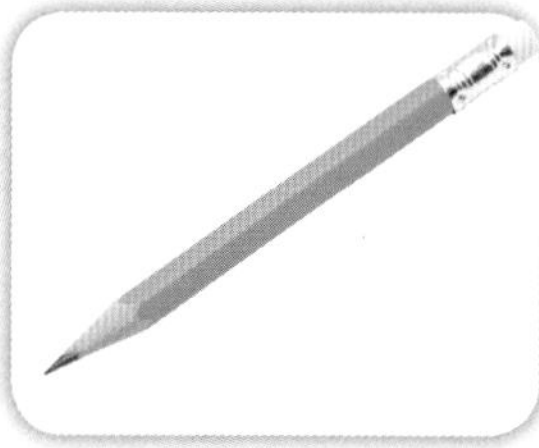

LESSON 5

LETTERS AND SOUNDS: Bb /b/, Pp /p/

1 TR: 1.11 Listen and point. **2** TR: 1.12 Listen. Trace and say. **3** TR: 1.13 Listen and chant. **4** TR: 1.14 Listen and match. Say.

A colourful house, Greece

A red train crossing a bridge, Germany

Big towers, Dubai

LESSON 6

VIDEO **Content Words:** *big, bridge, house, small, tower*

1 Look and see. **2** SC: 2 Watch. **3** SC: 2 Watch, point and say.

LESSON 7

PROJECT

1 Make.

Are you happy? UNIT 2

Happy girls, Pakistan

LESSON 1

NEW WORD: *happy*

1 Look and see. **2** SC: 3 Watch. **3** TR: 2.1 Listen and say. **4** TR: 2.2 Listen and do.

A girl, China

LESSON 2

NEW WORDS: *angry, excited, hungry, sad, sleepy, thirsty*

1 TR: 2.3 Listen and point. **2** TR: 2.4 Listen and say. **3** TR: 2.5 Listen and chant. **4** Do and say.

1

2

3

4

5

LESSON 3

STRUCTURE: *Are you happy? Yes, I am. Are you sad? No, I'm not.*

1 TR: 2.6 Listen and circle. **2** TR: 2.7 Listen and say. **3** Play and say.

A boy, India

A girl, Spain

Think! Value

Get a good night's sleep.

LESSON 4

SONG AND VALUE: *Get a good night's sleep.*

1 TR: 2.8 Listen and point. **2** TR: 2.9 Listen and sing. **3** TR: 2.10 Sing and do. **4** Stick.

Dd

Tt

LESSON 5

LETTERS AND SOUNDS: Dd /d/, Tt /t/

1 TR: 2.11 Listen and point. **2** TR: 2.12 Listen. Trace and say. **3** TR: 2.13 Listen and chant. **4** TR: 2.14 Listen and match. Say.

A boy playing the piano, Korea

LESSON 6

VIDEO **Content Words:** *loud, music, quiet*

1 Look and see. **2** SC: 4 Watch. **3** SC: 4 Watch and say.

LESSON 7

PROJECT

1 Make.

UNIT 3

Animals

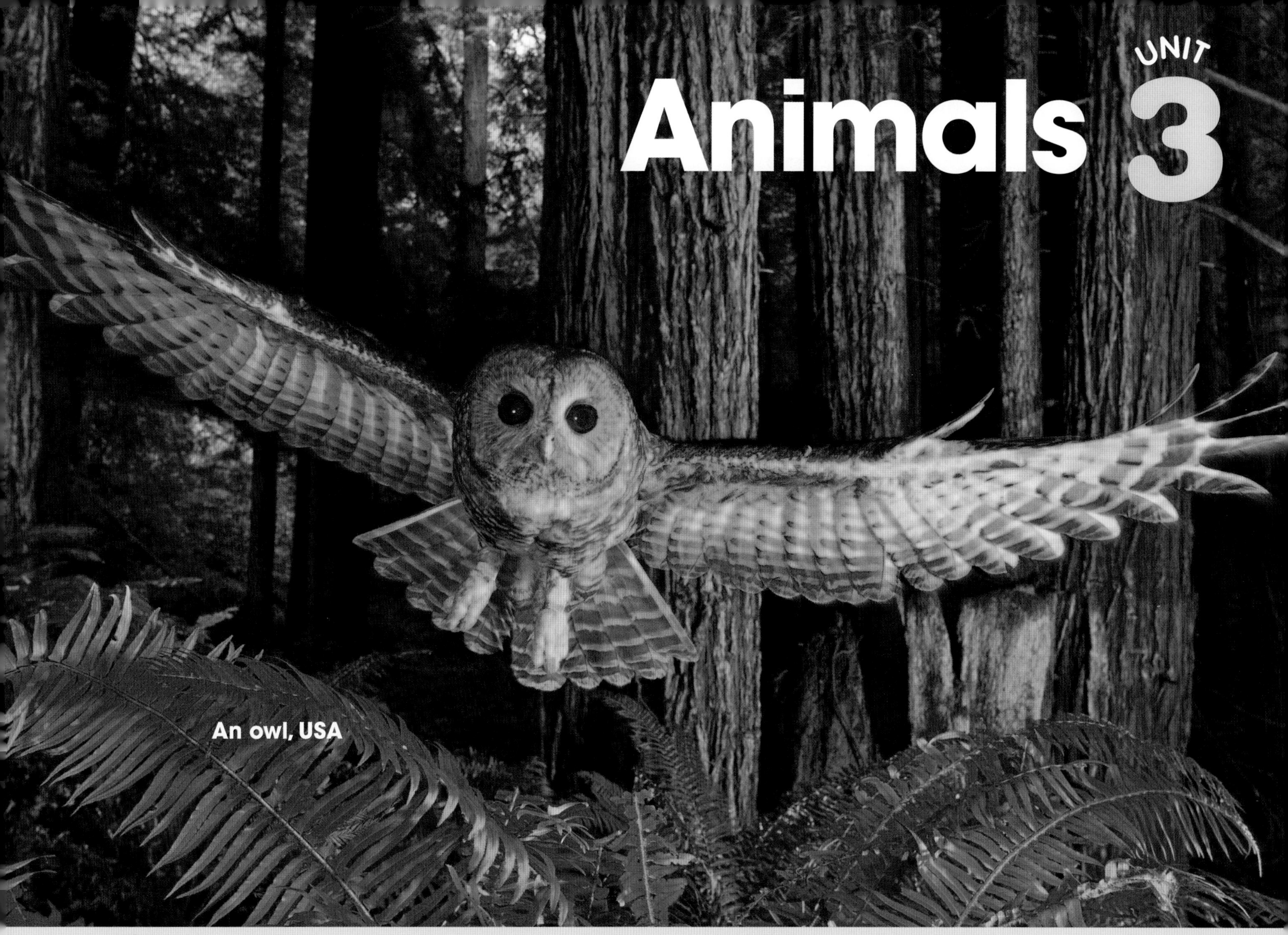

An owl, USA

LESSON 1

NEW WORD: *owl*

1 Look and see. **2** SC: 5 Watch. **3** TR: 3.1 Listen and say. **4** TR: 3.2 Listen and do.

LESSON 2

NEW WORDS: *bat, bear, duck, fox, rabbit, snake*

1 TR: 3.3 Listen and point. **2** TR: 3.4 Listen and say. **3** TR: 3.5 Listen and chant. **4** Draw and say.

LESSON 3

STRUCTURE: *What is it? It's an owl. What are they? They're bears.*

1 TR: 3.6 Listen and point. **2** TR: 3.7 Listen and say. **3** Play and say.

A bear, USA

LESSON 4

SONG AND VALUE: *Be curious about animals.*

1 TR: 3.8 Listen and point. **2** TR: 3.9 Listen and sing. **3** TR: 3.10 Sing and do. **4** Stick.

Think! Value

Be curious about animals.

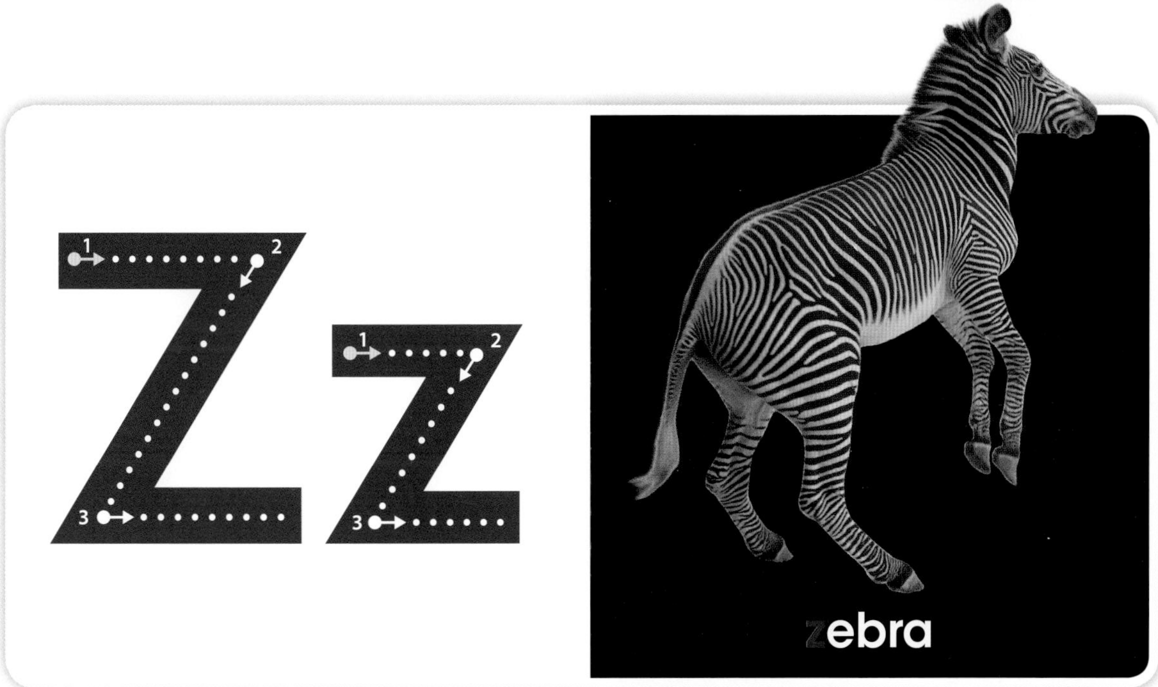

LESSON 5

LETTERS AND SOUNDS: Ss /s/, Zz /z/

1 TR: 3.11 Listen and point. **2** TR: 3.12 Listen. Trace and say. **3** TR: 3.13 Listen and chant. **4** TR: 3.14 Listen and match. Say.

A fox out at night and
ducks in the day

LESSON 6

VIDEO **Content Words:** *day, night*

1 Look and see. **2** SC: 6 Watch. **3** SC: 6 Watch and say.

LESSON 7

PROJECT

1 Make.

UNIT 4
Get dressed

A boy with his dog, Russia

LESSON 1

NEW WORD: *scarf*

1 Look and see. **2** SC: 7 Watch. **3** TR: 4.1 Listen and say. **4** TR: 4.2 Listen and do.

A girl in warm clothes, China

LESSON 2

NEW WORDS: *boots, coat, dress, jumper, skirt, trousers*

1 TR: 4.3 Listen and point. **2** TR: 4.4 Listen and say. **3** TR: 4.5 Listen and chant. **4** Find and say.

LESSON 3

STRUCTURE: *This is my jumper. These are my trousers.*

1 TR: 4.6 Listen and follow. **2** TR: 4.7 Listen and say. **3** Play and say.

Children wearing coats and boots, China

Think! Value

Dress for the weather.

LESSON 4

SONG AND VALUE: *Dress for the weather.*

1 TR: 4.8 Listen and point. **2** TR: 4.9 Listen and sing. **3** TR: 4.10 Sing and do. **4** Stick.

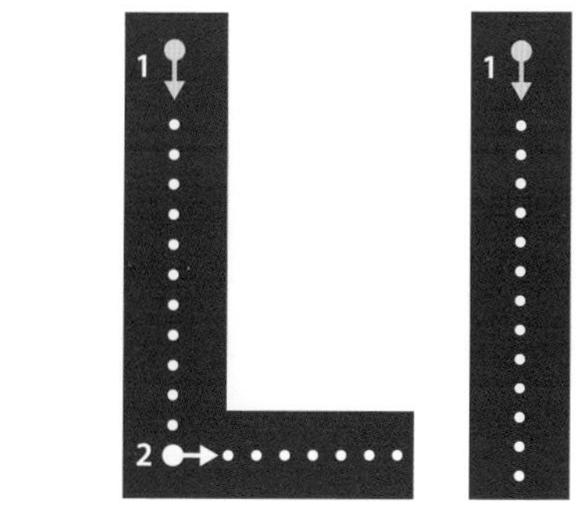

LESSON 5

LETTERS AND SOUNDS: Ll /l/, Rr /r/

1 TR: 4.11 Listen and point. **2** TR: 4.12 Listen. Trace and say. **3** TR: 4.13 Listen and chant. **4** TR: 4.14 Listen and match. Say.

LESSON 6

VIDEO **Content Words:** *cotton, plant, silk, worm*

1 Look and see. **2** SC: 8 Watch. **3** SC: 8 Watch and say.

LESSON 7

PROJECT

1 Make.

UNIT 5

I can jump!

Boys jumping in front of the Taj Mahal, India

LESSON 1

NEW WORD: *jump*

1 Look and see. **2** SC: 9 Watch. **3** TR: 5.1 Listen and say. **4** TR: 5.2 Listen and do.

Boy walking, Mexico

LESSON 2

NEW WORDS: *crawl, dance, hop, run, turn around, walk*

1 TR: 5.3 Listen and point. **2** TR: 5.4 Listen and say. **3** TR: 5.5 Listen and chant. **4** Say and do.

LESSON 3

STRUCTURE: *I can hop.*

1 TR: 5.6 Listen and point. **2** TR: 5.7 Listen and say. **3** Play and say.

Girls playing outside, Vietnam

Think! Value

Play outside.

LESSON 4

SONG AND VALUE: *Play outside.*

1 Look and see. **2** TR: 5.8 Listen and do. **3** TR: 5.9 Listen and sing. **4** Stick.

Mm

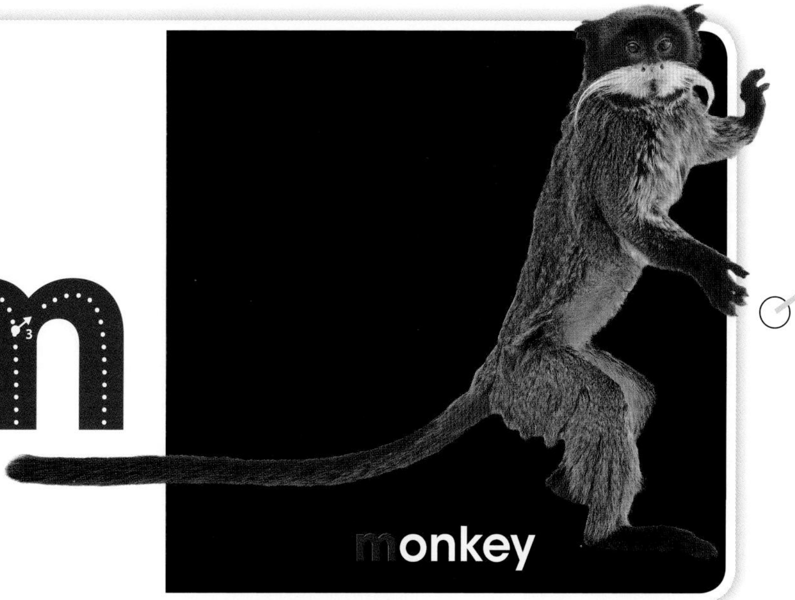

Nn

LESSON 5

LETTERS AND SOUNDS: Mm /m/, Nn /n/

1 TR: 5.10 Listen and point. **2** TR: 5.11 Listen. Trace and say. **3** TR: 5.12 Listen and chant. **4** TR: 5.13 Listen and match. Say.

A playground, USA

LESSON 6

VIDEO **Content Words:** *climb, hopscotch, playground*

1 Look and see. **2** SC: 10 Watch. **3** SC: 10 Watch and do.

LESSON 7

PROJECT

1 Make.

UNIT 6 Faces

Children with happy faces, Venezuela

LESSON 1

NEW WORD: *face*

1 Look and see. **2** SC: 11 Watch. **3** TR: 6.1 Listen and say. **4** TR: 6.2 Listen and do.

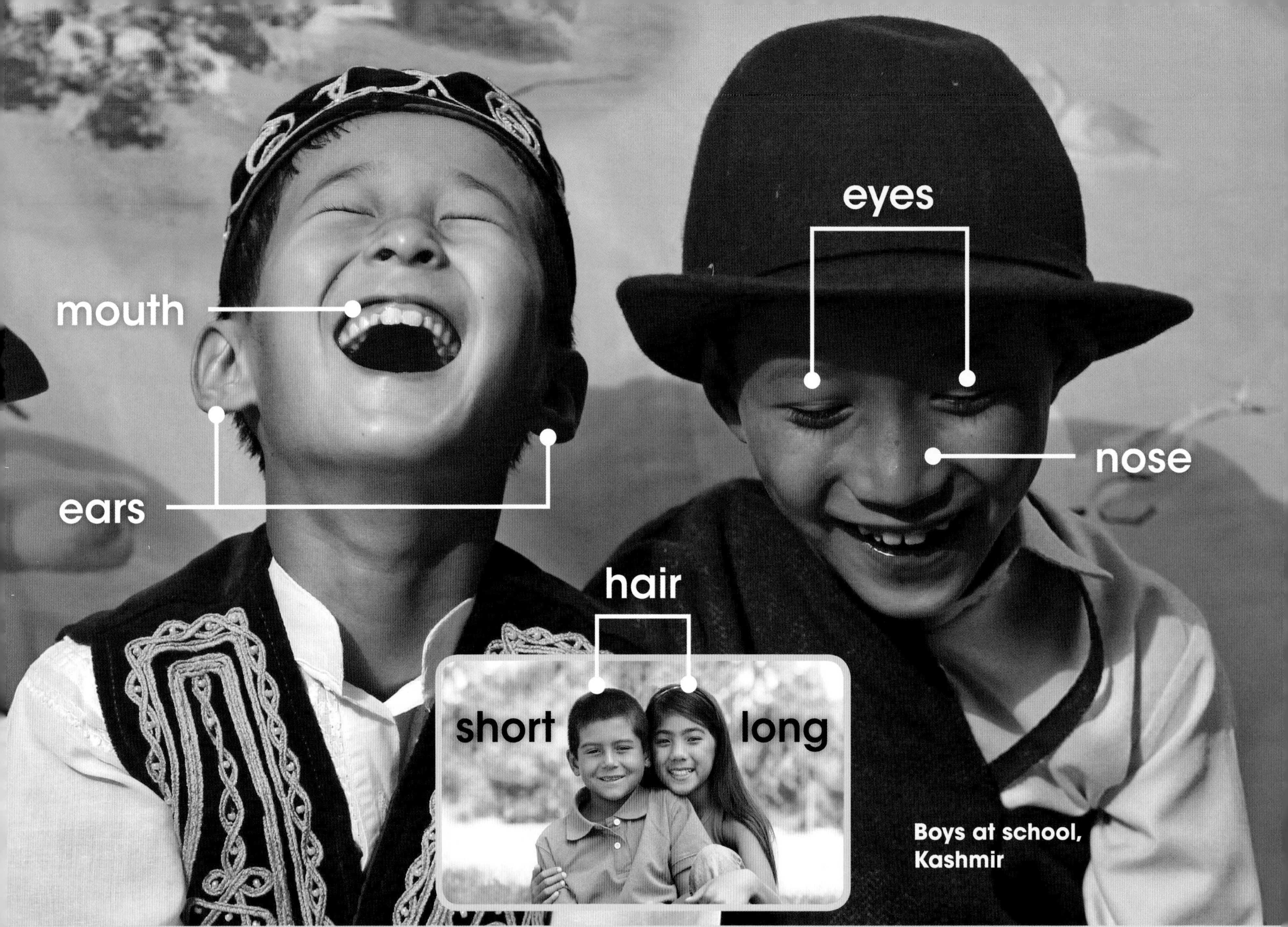

Boys at school, Kashmir

LESSON 2

NEW WORDS: *ears, eyes, hair, mouth, nose; long, short*

1 TR: 6.3 Listen and point. **2** TR: 6.4 Listen and say. **3** TR: 6.5 Listen and chant. **4** Touch and say.

LESSON 3

STRUCTURE: *He's got brown eyes. She's got long hair.*

1 TR: 6.6 Listen and point. **2** TR: 6.7 Listen and say. **3** Play and say.

A woman and a man, Norway

Children smiling, The Philippines

Think! Value

Say nice things.

LESSON 4

SONG AND VALUE: *Say nice things.*

1 TR: 6.8 Listen and point. **2** TR: 6.9 Listen and sing. **3** TR: 6.10 Sing and do. **4** Stick.

Gg

gorilla

Hh

hippo

LESSON 5

LETTERS AND SOUNDS: Gg /g/, Hh /h/

1 TR: 6.11 Listen and point. **2** TR: 6.12 Listen. Trace and say. **3** TR: 6.13 Listen and chant. **4** TR: 6.14 Listen and match. Say.

LESSON 6

VIDEO **Content Words:** *hear, sense, smell, taste*

1 Look and see. **2** SC:12 Watch. **3** SC:12 Watch, point and say.

LESSON 7

PROJECT

1 Make.

UNIT 7

My things

A boy with his dinosaurs, Italy

LESSON 1

NEW WORD: *dinosaur*

1 Look and see. **2** SC: 13 Watch. **3** TR: 7.1 Listen and say. **4** TR: 7.2 Listen and do.

LESSON 2

NEW WORDS: *bike, kite, puzzle, robot, scooter, tablet*

1 TR: 7.3 Listen and point. **2** TR: 7.4 Listen and say. **3** TR:7.5 Listen and chant. **4** Do and say.

LESSON 3

STRUCTURE: *Is this your kite? Yes, it is./No, it isn't.*

1 TR: 7.6 Listen and point. **2** TR: 7.7 Listen and say. **3** Play and say.

Girls playing with a bike and a scooter, Ukraine

Think! Value

Take turns.

LESSON 4

SONG AND VALUE: *Take turns.*

1 TR: 7.8 Listen and point. **2** TR: 7.9 Listen and sing. **3** TR:7.10 Sing and do. **4** Stick.

Cc

Qq

LESSON 5

LETTERS AND SOUNDS: Cc /k/, Qq /kw/

1 TR: 7.11 Listen and point. **2** TR: 7.12 Listen. Trace and say. **3** TR: 7.13 Listen and chant. **4** TR: 7.14 Listen and match. Say.

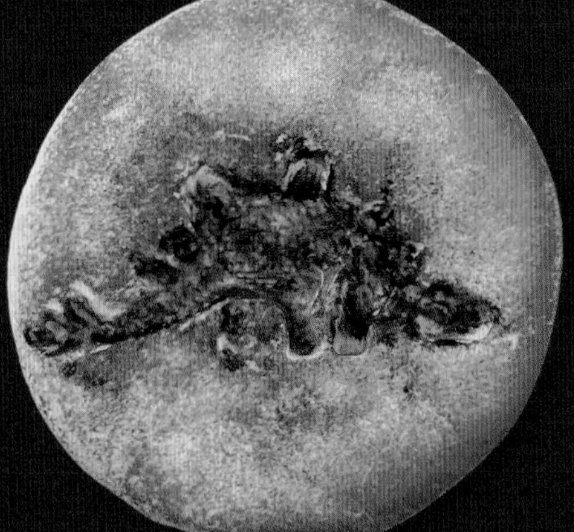

LESSON 6

VIDEO **Content Words:** *ground, neck, skeleton, tail*

1 Look and see. **2** SC: 14 Watch. **3** SC: 14 Watch, point and say.

LESSON 7

PROJECT

1 Make.

UNIT 8
Babies

A baby polar bear with its mother, Canada

LESSON 1

NEW WORD: *baby*

1 Look and see. **2** SC: 15 Watch. **3** TR: 8.1 Listen and say. **4** TR: 8.2 Listen and do.

Sheep in New Zealand

LESSON 2

NEW WORDS: *calf, chick, kitten, lamb, puppy; big, small*

1 TR: 8.3 Listen and point. **2** TR: 8.4 Listen and say. **3** TR: 8.5 Listen and chant. **4** Do and say.

LESSON 3

STRUCTURE: *There's one cow. There are two calves.*

1 TR: 8.6 Listen and point. **2** TR: 8.7 Listen and say. **3** Play and say.

Girl playing with puppies, Thailand

Think! Value

Be kind.

LESSON 4

SONG AND VALUE: *Be kind.*

1 TR: 8.8 Listen and point. **2** TR: 8.9 Listen and sing. **3** TR: 8.10 Sing and do. **4** Stick.

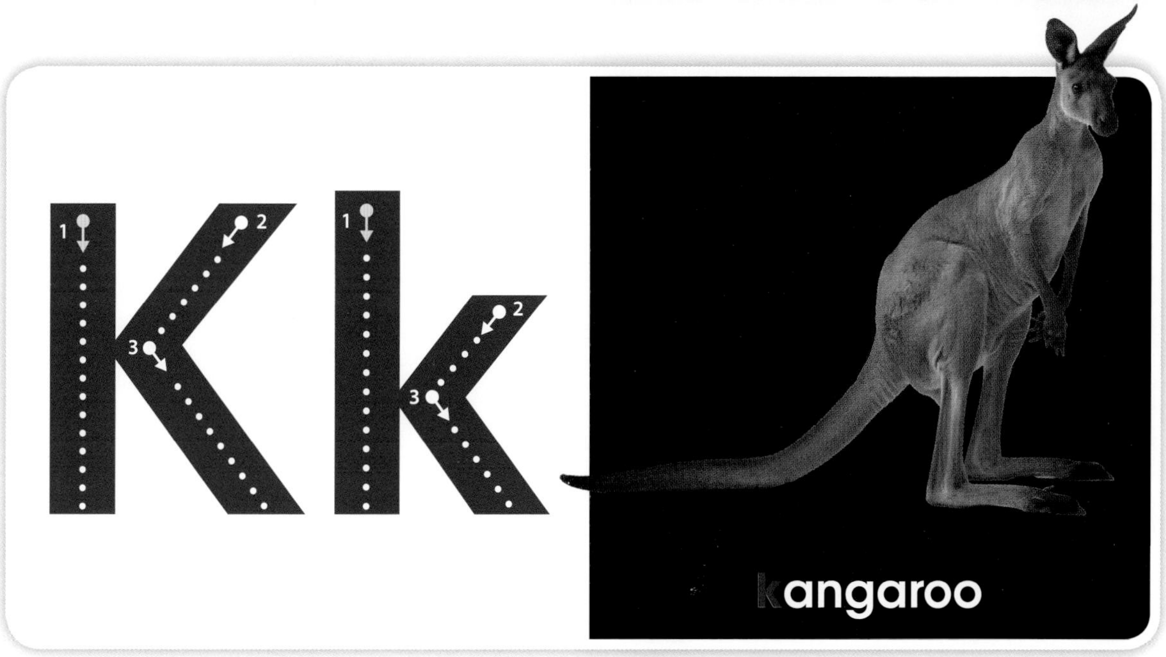

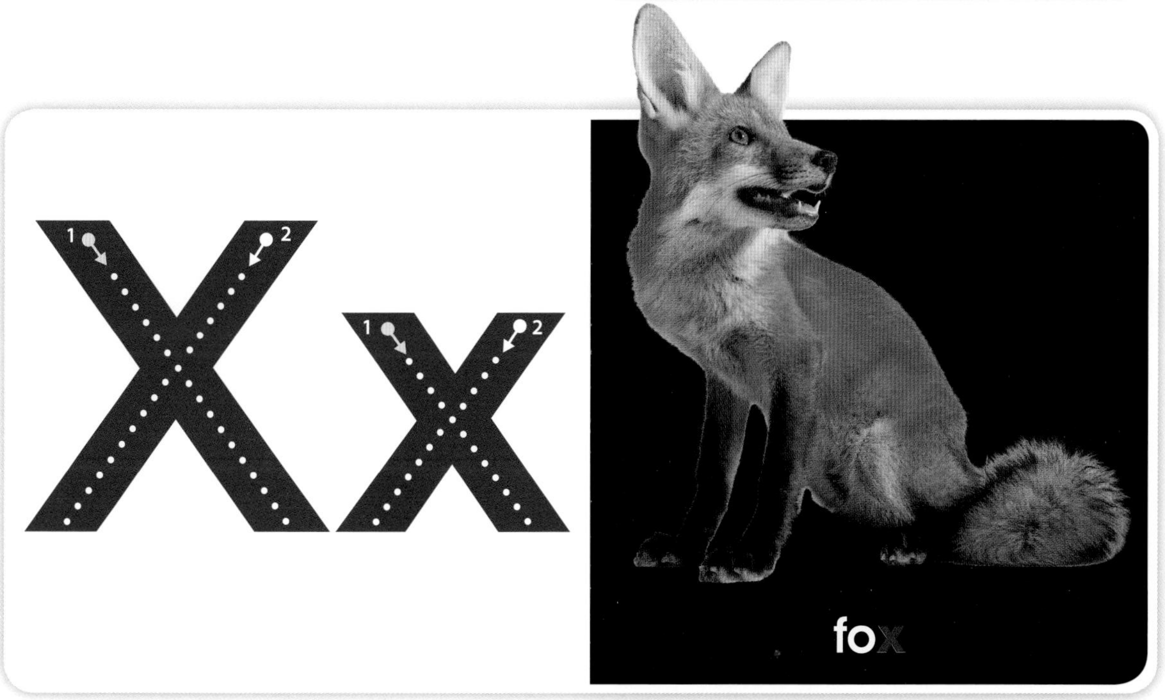

LESSON 5

LETTERS AND SOUNDS: Kk /k/, Xx /ks/

1 TR: 8.11 Listen and point. **2** TR: 8.12 Listen. Trace and say. **3** TR: 8.13 Listen and chant. **4** TR: 8.14 Listen and match. Say.

LESSON 6

VIDEO **Content Words:** *ant, egg, ostrich*

1 Look and see. **2** SC: 16 Watch. **3** SC: 16 Watch, point and say.

LESSON 7

PROJECT

1 Make.

UNIT 9

What's for dinner?

A man having dinner with his sons, Afghanistan

LESSON 1

NEW WORD: *dinner*

1 Look and see. **2** SC: 17 Watch. **3** TR: 9.1 Listen and say. **4** TR: 9.2 Listen and do.

LESSON 2

NEW WORDS: *beans, bread, chicken, fish, noodles, rice, salad*

1 TR: 9.3 Listen and point. **2** TR: 9.4 Listen and say. **3** TR: 9.5 Listen and chant. **4** Point and say.

LESSON 3

STRUCTURE: *What do you want? I want chicken, please.*

1 TR: 9.6 Listen and point. **2** TR: 9.7 Listen and say. **3** Tick (✔) and say.

Children helping in the kitchen, France

Think! Value

Help in the kitchen.

LESSON 4

SONG AND VALUE: *Help in the kitchen.*

1 TR: 9.8 Listen and point. **2** TR: 9.9 Listen and sing. **3** TR: 9.10 Sing and do. **4** Stick.

Jj

Yy

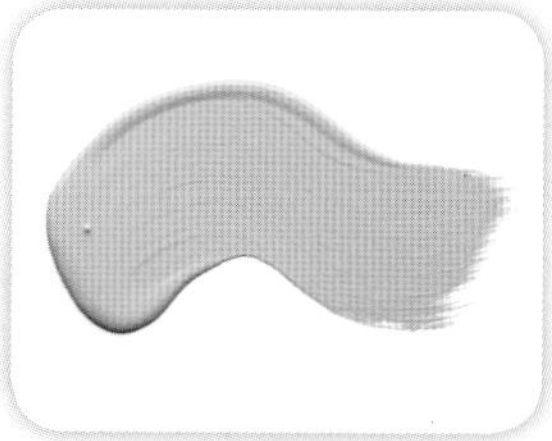

LESSON 5

LETTERS AND SOUNDS: Jj /dʒ/, Yy /j/

1 TR: 9.11 Listen and point. **2** TR: 9.12 Listen. Trace and say. **3** TR: 9.13 Listen and chant. **4** TR: 9.14 Listen and match. Say.

A woman making noodle soup, Thailand

LESSON 6

VIDEO **Content Words:** *cook, eat, onion, soup*

1 Look and see. **2** SC: 18 Watch. **3** SC: 18 Watch and say.

LESSON 7

PROJECT

1 Make.

UNIT 10 Insects

A Chinese peacock butterfly

LESSON 1

NEW WORD: *butterfly*

1 Look and see. **2** SC: 19 Watch. **3** TR: 10.1 Listen and say. **4** TR: 10.2 Listen and do.

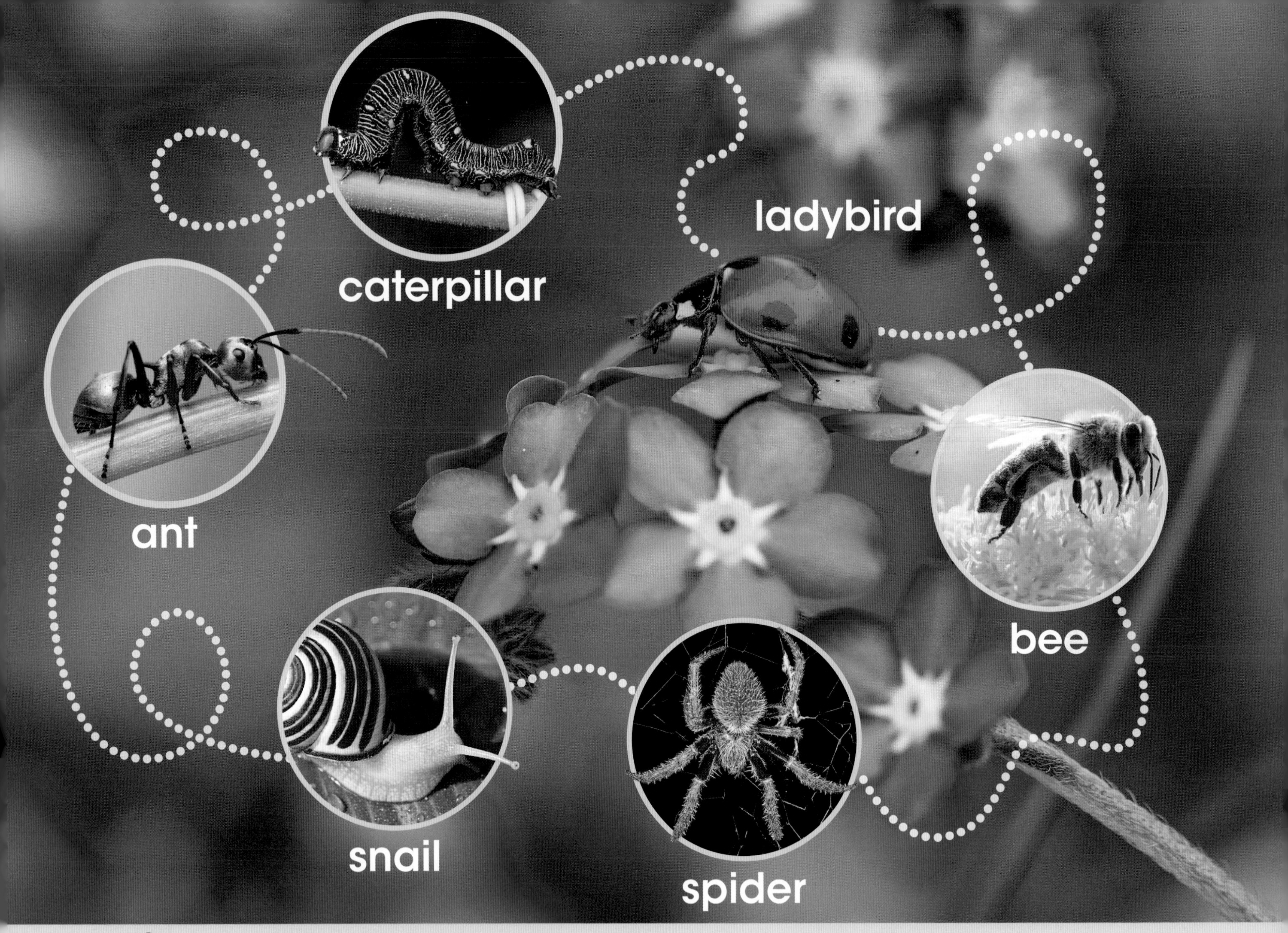

LESSON 2

NEW WORDS: *ant, bee, caterpillar, ladybird, snail, spider*

1 TR: 10.3 Listen and point. **2** TR: 10.4 Listen and say. **3** TR: 10.5 Listen and chant. **4** Draw and say.

LESSON 3

STRUCTURE: *Where's the caterpillar? It's on an apple.*

1 TR: 10.6 Listen and point. **2** TR: 10.7 Listen and say. **3** Play and say.

Think! Value

Be kind to nature.

LESSON 4

SONG AND VALUE: *Be kind to nature.*

1 TR: 10.8 Listen and point. **2** TR: 10.9 Listen and sing. **3** TR: 10.10 Sing and do. **4** Stick.

Ff

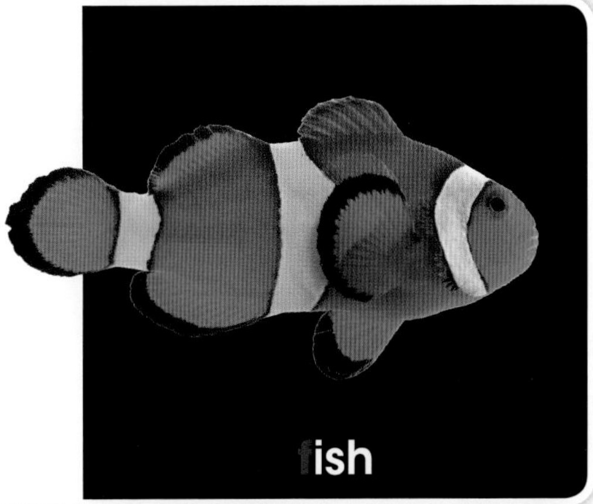

Vv

Ww

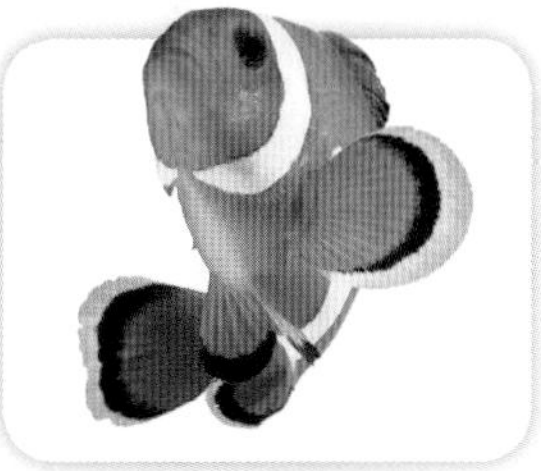

LESSON 5

LETTERS AND SOUNDS: Ff /f/, Vv /v/, Ww /w/

1 TR: 10.11 Listen and point. **2** TR: 10.12 Listen. Trace and say. **3** TR: 10.13 Listen and chant. **4** TR: 10.14 Listen and match. Say.

LESSON 7

PROJECT

1 Make.

LESSON 6

VIDEO **Content Word:** *pupa*

1 Look and see. **2** SC: 20 Watch. **3** SC: 20 Watch, point and say.

UNIT 1

At school

Look at the paper.
Look at the crayons.
Look at the pencils, too.

[Chorus]
Be tidy in the classroom.
Let's be tidy today.

Put away the paper.
Put away the crayons.
Put away the pencils, too.

[Chorus]

UNIT 2

Are you happy?

Are you happy?
No, I'm not.
Are you sad?
Yes, I am.
I'm sad and I'm sleepy.
He's sad and he's
sleepy today.

Don't be sad and sleepy.
Get a good night's sleep.

Are you excited?
No, I'm not.
Are you angry?
Yes, I am.
I'm angry and I'm sleepy.
She's angry and she's
sleepy today.

Don't be angry and sleepy.
Get a good night's sleep.

UNIT 4

Get dressed

These are my trousers.
These are my boots.
This is my coat
and this is my hat.
These are my clothes.
I'm ready to play.
I'm dressed for the
cold weather.

This is my T-shirt.
These are my shorts.
This is my hat
and these are my shoes.
These are my clothes.
I'm ready to play.
I'm dressed for the
hot weather.

UNIT 3

Animals

What is it?
It's a bear.
It's a big bear.
What colour is it?
It's brown.
It's a big, brown bear.

[Chorus]
Let's learn about animals.
Let's be curious.

What are they?
They're bats.
They're small bats.
What colour are they?
They're brown.
They're small, brown bats.

[Chorus]

UNIT 5

I can jump!

I can hop and I can crawl.
I can crawl and I can run.
Let's play outside. It's so fun.
Let's hop and crawl and run!

I can jump and I can dance.
I can dance and I can run.
Let's play outside. It's so fun.
Let's jump and dance and run!

I can walk and I can hop.
I can hop and I can run.
Let's play outside. It's so fun.
Let's walk and hop and run!

UNIT 6

Faces

This is my sister.
She's got brown hair.
This is my dad.
He's got brown hair, too.

[Chorus]
What a nice photo!
I like your photo.
Thank you, thank you!
It's good to say nice things!

This is my sister.
She's got brown eyes.
This is my friend.
She's got brown eyes, too.

[Chorus]

UNIT 7

My things

Is this your bike?
Yes, it is. It's my new bike.
Can I see it?
It's very nice.
I like your nice, new bike!

[Chorus]
Here you are.
Let's take turns.
Let's take turns and play.

Is this your scooter?
Yes, it is. It's my new scooter.
Can I see it?
It's very nice.
I like your nice, new scooter!

[Chorus]

UNIT 8

Babies

There's one puppy -
one small puppy.
It's a sad puppy.
One small, sad puppy.
Let's be kind to the puppy.
Let's play and have fun.
Now there's a happy puppy.
He's a happy one!

There are two puppies -
two small puppies.
They're sad puppies.
Two small, sad puppies.
Let's be kind to the puppies.
Let's play and have fun.
Now there are two
happy puppies.
That's better than one!

UNIT 9

What's for dinner?

What do you want for
dinner today?
What do you want for dinner?
I want chicken and
noodles, please.
I want eggs, too.

[Chorus]
Let's help in the kitchen.
Let's make dinner today.

What do you want for
dinner today?
What do you want for dinner?
I want fish and rice, please.
I want beans, too.

[Chorus]

What do you want for
dinner today?
What do you want for dinner?
I want eggs and bread, please.
I want salad, too.

[Chorus]

UNIT 10

Insects

What's this?
It's an ant.
Where's the ant?
It's on a leaf.
It's happy on its leaf.

Look and see,
but don't touch me!
I'm happy on my leaf.

What's this?
It's a bee.
Where's the bee?
It's on a flower.
It's happy on its flower.

Look and see,
but don't touch me!
I'm happy on my flower.

What's this?
It's a snail.
Where's the snail?
It's on a tree.
It's happy on its tree.

Look and see,
but don't touch me!
I'm happy on my tree.

Aa

alligator

Bb

beaver

Cc

camel

Dd

duck

Ii

iguana

Jj

jaguar

Kk

kangaroo

Ll

lion

Qq

quail

Rr

reindeer

Ss

seal

Tt

tiger

Uu

umbrellabird

Ee

elephant

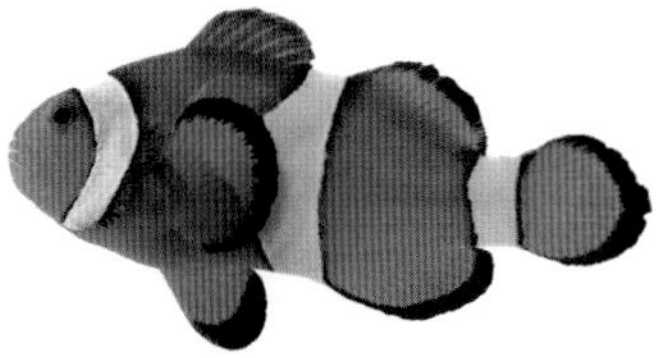

Ff

fish

Gg

gorilla

Hh

hippo

Mm

monkey

Nn

numbat

Oo

octopus

Pp

panda

Vv

vulture

Ww

wolf

Xx

fo**x**

Yy

yak

Zz

zebra

CREDITS

PHOTOS: 2 (t) Majority World CIC/Danita Delimont Stock Photography; (mt) Athar Hussain/Reuters; (m) Michael Nichols/National Geographic Image Collection; (mb) © Revodana Publishing/www.littlekidsbigdogs.com; (b) © David Lazar; **3** (t) Juan Silva/The Image Bank/Getty Images; (mt) Gabriele Galimberti and Juri de Luca/National Geographic Image Collection; (m) ©Nadeem Sufi; (mb) Paula Lerner/Aurora Photos/Cavan Images; (b) RGB Ventures/Alamy Stock Photo; **4** (tl) Sergiy Tryapitsyn/Alamy Stock Photo; (tm) Peter Dazeley/Photographer's Choice/Getty Images; (tr, mtr, mbr, br) Joel Sartore/National Geographic Image Collection; (mtl) recebin/Shutterstock.com; (mtm) prochasson frederic/Shutterstock.com; (ml) Chayapon Bootboonneam/EyeEm/Getty Images; (mm) Chris Winsor/Moment/Getty Images; (mr) Joel Sartore, National Geographic Photo Ark/National Geographic Image Collection; (mbl) Mega Pixel/Shutterstock.com; (mbm) Olhastock/Shutterstock.com; (bl) Anna Kucherova/Shutterstock.com; (bm) Super Prin/Shutterstock.com; (background) Lumikk555/Shutterstock.com; **5** Majority World CIC/Danita Delimont Stock Photography; **6** (l) Hero Images/Getty Images; (m) Fototocam/Shutterstock.com; (r) Mega Pixel/Shutterstock.com; (background) © Maria Manco Photography; **8** © Matt Moyer; **9** (tl, bl) Joel Sartore, National Geographic Photo Ark/National Geographic Image Collection; (tr) chalrumpon onnongwa/Shutterstock.com; (mtr) Sergey Ivanychev/EyeEm/Getty Images; (mr) Jody Ann/Shutterstock.com; (bmr) Eric Isselee/Shutterstock.com; (br) KasperczakBohdan/Shutterstock.com; **10** (tl) Joana Kruse/AGE Fotostock; (r) Rostislav Kralik/Alamy Stock Photo; (bl) Loetscher Chlaus/Alamy Stock Photo; (project) © 2021 Cengage; **11** Athar Hussain/Reuters; **12** (tl) Tetyana Kaganska/Shutterstock.com; (tm) Victoria Penafiel/Moment/Getty Images; (tr) PhotoAlto/Belen Majdalani/PhotoAlto Agency RF Collections/Getty Images; (m) Laura Olivas/Moment/Getty Images; (b) Aguru/E+/Getty Images; (background) Wu Jibin Xinhua/eyevine/Redux; **13** (tl) wavebreakmedia/Shutterstock.com; (tm) sudo takeshi/Taxi/Getty Images; (tr) Maria Symchych/Shutterstock.com; (bl) Jajmo/iStock/Getty Images; (bm) Sofie Delauw/Cultura/Getty Images; (background) pockygallery/Shutterstock.com; **14** (l) PhotosIndia.com/photosindia/Getty Images; (r) Westend61/Getty Images; **15** (tl) Joel Sartore, National Geographic Photo Ark/National Geographic Image Collection; (tr) Eric Isselee/Shutterstock.com; (mtr) CykOtie/Shutterstock.com; (mr) mari_art/iStock/Getty Images; (bl) Joel Sartore/National Geographic Image Collection; (mbr) flowgraph/Shutterstock.com; (br) Aksenova Natalya/Shutterstock.com; **16** Masterfile; (project) © 2021 Cengage; **17** Michael Nichols/National Geographic Image Collection; **18** (tl) Dave Montreuil/Shutterstock.com; (tr) NaturesThumbPrint/iStock/Getty Images; (m) Luka Hercigonja/Shutterstock.com; (bl) K Quinn Ferris/Shutterstock.com; (br) Menno Schaefer/Shutterstock.com; (background) © Olivier Colle/Comedy Wildlife Photography Awards; **20** (t) Charlie Hamilton James/National Geographic Image Collection; (b) Lillian Tveit/Shutterstock.com; (project) © 2021 Cengage; **21** (tl, bl) Joel Sartore, National Geographic Photo Ark/National Geographic Image Collection; (tr) Martin Christopher Parker/Shutterstock.com; (mtr) kali9/E+/Getty Images; (mr) Africa Studio/Shutterstock.com; (mbr) Lucas T. Jahn/Shutterstock.com; (br) Johan Larson/Shutterstock.com; **22** (l) Courtesy Tomasz Kowalski; (r) Jim Nelson/EyeEm/Getty Images; (project) © 2021 Cengage; (tl) Javier Fernández Sánchez/Moment/Getty Images; (tr) 945ontwerp/E+/Getty Images; (bl) narayankumar/iStock/Getty Images; (br) FotoRequest/Shutterstock.com; **23** © Revodana Publishing/www.littlekidsbigdogs.com; **24** (tl) Oxa/Shutterstock.com; (tr) Tarzhanova/Shutterstock.com; (m) windu/Shutterstock.com; (bl) Magdalena Wielobob/Shutterstock.com; (br) Ruslan Kudrin/Shutterstock.com; (background) Xuanyu Han/Moment/Getty Images; **26** (l) Kim Kyung-Hoon/Reuters; (r) ArtMarie/E+/Getty Images; **27** (tl, bl) Joel Sartore, National Geographic Photo Ark/National Geographic Image Collection; (tr) Giedriius/Shutterstock.com; (mtr) Fotofermer/Shutterstock.com; (mr) Vera Larina/Shutterstock.com; (mbr) Eric Isselee/Shutterstock.com; (br) Floortje/iStock/Getty Images; **28** (l) Yogesh Mohite/EyeEm/Getty Images; (r) Natalie Fobes/The Image Bank/Getty Images; (project) © 2021 Cengage; **29** © David Lazar; **30** (tl) Felix Mizioznikov/Shutterstock.com; (tr) Elizabethsalleebauer/RooM/Getty Images; (ml) MoMorad/E+/Getty Images; (mr) TheVisualsYouNeed/Shutterstock.com; (b) David Patrick Valera/Moment/Getty Images; (background) RooM the Agency/Alamy Stock Photo; **32** © Henry Lee; **33** (tl, bl) Joel Sartore, National Geographic Photo Ark/National Geographic Image Collection; (tr) Pollyana Ventura/E+/Getty Images; (mtr) Jiri Hera/Shutterstock.com; (mr) Eric Isselee/Shutterstock.com; (mbr) meyblume/Shutterstock.com; (br) dubassy/Shutterstock.com; **34** © D. James Dee; (project) © 2021 Cengage; **35** Juan Silva/The Image Bank/Getty Images; **36** (t) Fayaz Kabli/Reuters; (b) MBI/Alamy Stock Photo; **37** (tl) rSnapshotPhotos/Shutterstock.com; (tml) Dima Sidelnikov/Shutterstock.com; (tmr, bmr) Jose Luis Pelaez Inc/DigitalVision/Getty Images; (tr) HKPNC/iStock/Getty Images; (bl) Morsa Images/DigitalVision/Getty Images; (bml) QTGraemes Photography/Moment/Getty Images; (br) Epiximages/iStock/Getty Images; (background) YamabikaY/Shutterstock.com; **38** (l) Erika Larsen/National Geographic Image Collection; (r) Alain Evrard/Robert Harding; (background) Axel Bueckert/EyeEm/Getty Images; **39** (tl) bl) Joel Sartore, National Geographic Photo Ark/National Geographic Image Collection; (tr) Cat'chy Images/Shutterstock.com; (mtr) Anurak Pongpatimet/Shutterstock.com; (mr) Anan Kaewkhammul/Shutterstock.com; (mbr) vitaliy_73/Shutterstock.com; (br) Aaron Amat/Shutterstock.com; **40** (tl) Stefan Holm/Alamy Stock Photo; (tm) Pakin Songmor/Moment/Getty Images; (tr) Mike Bons/500px/Getty Images; (bl) Martin Jeffries/500px Prime/Getty Images; (br) Vaivirga/Alamy Stock Photo; (project) © 2021 Cengage; **41** Gabriele Galimberti and Juri de Luca/National Geographic Image Collection; **42** (t) Heidi Becker/Shutterstock.com; (ml) Hurst Photo/Shutterstock.com; (mr) time4studio/Shutterstock.com; (bl) Monthira/Shutterstock.com; (br) CGinspiration/E+/Getty Images; (background) Besjunior/iStock/Getty Images; **44** Sinenkiy/iStock/Getty Images; **45** (tl, bl) Joel Sartore, National Geographic Photo Ark/National Geographic Image Collection; (tr) Matteo Fagiolino/Moment/Getty Images; (mtr) achiaos/Shutterstock.com; (mr) nitat/Shutterstock.com; (mbr) Chalabala/iStock/Getty Images; (br) Westend61/Getty Images; **46** (tl) ullstein bild/Getty Images; (r) Raymond Warren/Alamy Stock Photo; (bl) Hemis/Alamy Stock Photo; (project) © 2021 Cengage; **47** ©Nadeem Sufi; **48** (l) Adam Gryko/Shutterstock.com; (ml) PCHT/Shutterstock.com; (mr) Katho Menden/Shutterstock.com; (r) Grigorita Ko/Shutterstock.com; (background) robertharding/Alamy Stock Photo; **49** (tl, mtl, bl) Eric Isselee/Shutterstock.com; (tm) Ramona Heim/Shutterstock.com; (tr) S-F/Shutterstock.com; (trb) Kuttelvaserova Stuchelova/Shutterstock.com; (mtr) Cherry-Merry/Shutterstock.com; (ml) photomaster/Shutterstock.com; (mr) Diane Kuhl/Shutterstock.com; (mbl) Tsekhmister/Shutterstock.com; (mbr) Erik Lam/Shutterstock.com; (br) MirasWonderland/Shutterstock.com; (background) primopiano/Shutterstock.com; **50** (t) Sarawut Intarob/Getty Images; (bl) Tierfotoagentur/Alamy Stock Photo; **51** (tl, bl) Joel Sartore, National Geographic Photo Ark/National Geographic Image Collection; (tr) Thatsaniya Thawongklang/Shutterstock.com; (mtr) Lubava/Shutterstock.com; (mr) Bradley Blackburn/Shutterstock.com; (mbr) Nikographer [Jon]/Flickr RF/Getty Images; (br) Hurst Photo/Shutterstock.com; **52** (tl) Arto Hakola/Getty Images; (tr) Aukid Phumsirichat/EyeEm/Getty Images; (ml) phasinphoto/Getty Images; (mm) sruilk/Shutterstock.com; (mr) Wildlife Gmbh/Alamy Stock Photo; (b) WaterFrame/Alamy Stock Photo; (project) © 2021 Cengage; Heiko Kiera/Shutterstock.com; **53** Paula Lerner/Aurora Photos/Cavan Images; **54** (tl) Maria Uspenskaya/Shutterstock.com; (tr) Eugene Mymrin/Moment/Getty Images; (bl) Anna_Pustynnikova/Shutterstock.com; (br) Aleksandra Berzhets/Shutterstock.com; (background) Elena Veselova/Alamy Stock Photo; **55** (tl) AS Food studio/Shutterstock.com; (tm) Yaruniv Studio/Shutterstock.com; (tr) Edalin Photography/Shutterstock.com; (ml) Jantima14/Shutterstock.Com; (mr) Valerio Pardi/Shutterstock.com; (bl) Goffkein.Pro/Shutterstock.com; (bml) Tatiana Volgutova/Shutterstock.com; (bmr) Jiri Hera/Shutterstock.com; (br) Timolina/Shutterstock.com; (foreground: l, r) David M. Schrader/Shutterstock.com; (foreground: m) EllenM/Shutterstock.com; (background) Nelson garrido Silva/Shutterstock.com; **56** (tl) Tatiana Bralnina/Shutterstock.com; (tm) Timolina/Shutterstock.com; (tr) Claudia Totir/Moment/Getty Images; (b) Lambert Simon/Haytham-Rea/Redux; **57** (tl, bl) Joel Sartore, National Geographic Photo Ark/National Geographic Image Collection; (tr) Superstock/Alamy Stock Photo; (mtr) Karkas/Shutterstock.com; (mr) Eric Isselee/Shutterstock.com; (mbr) Johnnie Pakington/Moment/Getty Images; (br) JackF/iStock/Getty Images; **58** AJP/Shutterstock.com; (project) © 2021 Cengage; **59** RGB Ventures/Alamy Stock Photo; **60** (t) George Grall/National Geographic Image Collection; (ml) Rundstedt B. Rovillos/Moment/Getty Images; (mr) Helmut Seisenberger/Moment/Getty Images; (bl) Klaus Vartzbed/EyeEm/Getty Images; (br) Arto Hakola/Moment/Getty Images; (background) mikroman6/Moment/Getty Images; **61** (tl) Jacky Parker Photography/Moment/Getty Images; (tr) timmy/iStock/Getty Images; (ml) ET1972/Shutterstock.com; (mr) Teddi Yaeger Photography/Moment/Getty Images; (bl) Annette Perrio/EyeEm/Getty Images; (br) Rastislav Profant/500px Prime/Getty Images; (background) Gareth Dabell/EyeEm/Getty Images; **62** (l) Matthias Lenke/Science Source; (m) Philippe Lejeanvre/Moment/Getty Images; (r) Roman Alyabev/EyeEm/Getty Images; **63** (tl, ml) Joel Sartore, National Geographic Photo Ark/National Geographic Image Collection; (tr) Luis Echeverri Urrea/Shutterstock.com; (mtr) mariait/Shutterstock.com; (mr) bluehand/Shutterstock.com; (bl) Joel Sartore/National Geographic Image Collection; (mbr) punkbirdr/Shutterstock.com; (br) Syda Productions/Shutterstock.com; **64** (tl) Breck P. Kent/Shutterstock.com; (tr) Brandon Alms/Shutterstock.com; (bl) Straublund Photography/Moment/Getty Images; (br) Rolf Nussbaumer/Minden Pictures; (project) © 2021 Cengage; **65** (l) © Matt Moyer; (r) PhotosIndia.com/photosindia/Getty Images; **66** (l) Charlie Hamilton James/National Geographic Image Collection; (r) Kim Kyung-Hoon/Reuters; **67** (l) © Henry Lee; (r) Alain Evrard/Robert Harding; **68** (l) Sinenkiy/iStock/Getty Images; (r) Sarawut Intarob/500px Prime/Getty Images; **69** (l) Lambert Simon/Haytham-Rea/Redux; (r) Philippe Lejeanvre/Moment/Getty Images; **70** (all) Joel Sartore/National Geographic Photo Ark/National Geographic Image Collection; **71** (all) Joel Sartore/National Geographic Photo Ark/National Geographic Image Collection; **Back Cover** Joel Sartore/National Geographic Image Collection.

ILLUSTRATIONS: All mascot artwork created by Fabiana Faiallo; **7, 8, 14, 20, 26, 32, 38, 44, 50, 56, 62** Fabiana Faiallo; **19, 25, 31, 43** Jill Dubin/Painted Words, Claire Easton.